SCHOLASTIC

writing guides

With interactive resources on CD-ROM

Adventure Stories

for ages
7-9

Pam Dowson
and
Guy Merchant

C000260549

Credits

Authors
Pam Dowson and
Guy Merchant

Development Editors
Rachel Mackinnon and
Marion Archer

Assistant Editor
Sarah Sodhi

Series Designer
Anna Oliwa

Designers
Paul Stockmans and
Liz Gilbert

Cover Illustration
Mark Oliver

Illustrations
Garry Davies

CD-ROM Development
CD-ROM developed in
association with Infuze Ltd

Mixed Sources
Product group from well-managed
forests and other controlled sources
www.fsc.org Cert no. TT-COC-002769
© 1996 Forest Stewardship Council

Text © 2010, Pam Dowson
Text © 2002, 2010 Guy Merchant
© 2010 Scholastic Ltd

Designed using Adobe InDesign

Published by Scholastic Ltd,
Book End,
Range Road,
Witney,
Oxfordshire
OX29 0YD

www.scholastic.co.uk

Printed by Bell & Bain

1 2 3 4 5 6 7 8 9   0 1 2 3 4 5 6 7 8 9

British Library Cataloguing-in-Publication Data
A catalogue record for this book is available from the British Library.

ISBN 978-1407-11250-3

Acknowledgments
The publisher gratefully acknowledge permission to reproduce the following copyright material: **AM Heath & Co Ltd** for the use of an extract from *The Secret World of Polly Flint* by Helen Cresswell © 1983, Helen Cresswell (1983, Puffin). Every effort has been made to trace copyright holders for the works reproduced in this book, and the publishers apologise for any inadvertent omissions.

CD-ROM Minimum specifications:

Windows 2000/XP/Vista	Mac OSX 10.4	
Processor: 1 GHz	RAM: 512 MB	Graphics card: 32bit
Audio card: Yes	CD-ROM drive speed: 8x	Hard disk space: 200MB
Screen resolution: 800x600		

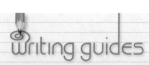

Contents

4 Introduction

5 How to use the CD-ROM

Section 1: Using good examples

7 Teachers' notes

Photocopiable extracts 1–3
10 The Catcher
11 So Near...
12 Joby and the Wasters

Photocopiable activities
14 Who was that?
15 Time to decide
16 Story detectives
17 How does it feel?
18 Adventure soup

Section 2: Developing writing

19 Teachers' notes

Photocopiable activities
25 Adventure ideas
26 Adventure maps
27 Pull the trigger
28 Cliffhangers
29 An element of surprise
30 Meanwhile...

31 Should I stay or should I go?
32 Road rage
33 On location
34 Seeing stars

Section 3: Writing

35 Teachers' notes

Photocopiable activities
38 Story planner
40 Dangerous quest
41 The confrontation
42 Race to the finish
43 Vital equipment

Section 4: Review

44 Teachers' notes

Photocopiable activities
45 Self review
46 Peer review
47 Teacher review

Introduction: Adventure Stories

The *Writing Guides* series aims to inspire and motivate children as writers by using creative approaches. Each *Writing Guide* contains activities and photocopiable resources designed to develop children's understanding of a particular genre (for example, fairy stories). The activities are in line with the requirements of the National Curriculum and the recommendations in the *Primary Framework for Literacy*. The teacher resource books are accompanied by a CD-ROM containing a range of interactive activities and resources.

What's in the book?

The *Writing Guides* series provides a structured approach to developing children's writing. Each book is divided into four sections.

Section 1: **Using good examples**
Three text extracts are provided to explore the typical features of the genre.

Section 2: **Developing writing**
There are ten short, focussed writing tasks in this section. These are designed to develop children's ability to use the key features of the genre in their own writing. The teachers' notes explain the objective of each activity and provide guidance on delivery, including how to use the photocopiable pages and the materials on the CD-ROM.

Section 3: **Writing**
The three writing projects in this section require the children to produce an extended piece of writing using the key features of the genre.

Section 4: **Review**
This section consists of a 'Self review', 'Peer review' and 'Teacher review'. These can be used to evaluate how effectively the children have met the writing criteria for the genre.

What's on the CD-ROM?

The accompanying CD-ROM contains a range of motivating activities and resources. The activities can be used for independent work or can be used on an interactive whiteboard to enhance group teaching.
Each CD-ROM contains:

- three text extracts that illustrate the typical features of the genre
- interactive versions of selected photocopiable pages
- four photographs and an audio file to create imaginative contexts for writing
- a selection of writing templates and images which can be used to produce extended pieces of writing.

The interactive activities on the CD-ROM promote active learning and support a range of teaching approaches and learning styles. For example, drag and drop and sequencing activities will support kinaesthetic learners.

Talk for writing

Each *Writing Guide* uses the principles of 'Talk for writing' to support children's writing development by providing opportunities for them to rehearse ideas orally in preparation for writing. 'Talk for writing' is promoted using a variety of teaching strategies including discussions, questioning and drama activities (such as, developing imaginative dialogue – see *Fantasy Stories for Ages 9–11*).

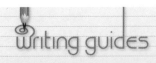

How to use the CD-ROM

Start screen: click on the 'Start' button to go to the main menu.

This section contains brief instructions on how to use the CD-ROM. For more detailed guidance, go to 'How to use the CD-ROM' on the start screen or click on the 'Help' button located in the top right-hand corner of the screen.

Installing the CD-ROM

Follow the instructions on the disk to install the CD-ROM onto your computer. Once the CD-ROM is installed, navigate to the program location and double click on the program icon to open it.

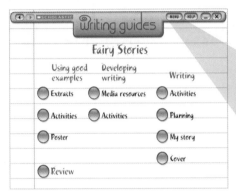

Main menu screen

Main menu

The main menu provides links to all of the writing activities and resources on the CD-ROM. Clicking on a button from the main menu will take you to a sub-menu that lists all of the activities and resources in that section. From here you have the option to 'Launch' the interactive activities, which may contain more than one screen, or print out the activities for pupils to complete by hand.

If you wish to return to a previous menu, click the 'Menu' button in the top right-hand corner of the screen; this acts as a 'back' button.

Screen tools

A range of simple writing tools that can be used in all of the writing activities are contained in the toolbar at the bottom of the screen.

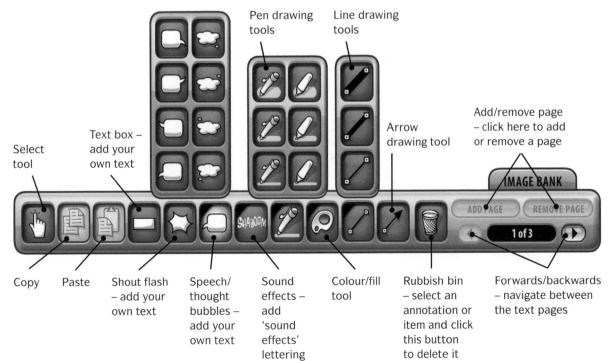

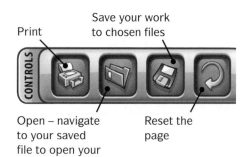

Print

Save your work to chosen files

Open – navigate to your saved file to open your previous work

Reset the page

Printing and saving work

All of the resources on the CD-ROM are printable. You can also save and retrieve any annotations made on the writing activities. Click on the 'Controls' tab on the right-hand side of the screen to access the 'Print', 'Open', 'Save' and 'Reset screen' buttons.

View all thumbnails by clicking on the arrows

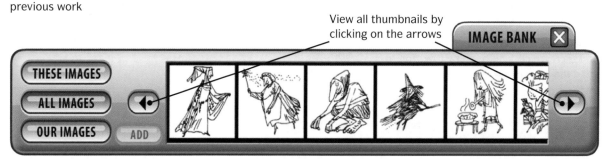

Image bank – click and drag an image to add it to an activity

Image bank

Each CD-ROM has an 'Image bank' containing images appropriate to the genre being taught. Click on the tab at the bottom right of the screen to open the 'Image bank'. On the left-hand side there are three large buttons.

- The 'These images' button will display only the images associated with the specific activity currently open.
- The 'All images' button will display all the photographs and illustrations available on the CD-ROM.
- The 'Our images' button will contain any images you or the children have added to the CD-ROM.

Press the left or right arrows to scroll through the images available. Select an image and drag and drop it into the desired location on the screen. If necessary, resize the image using the arrow icon that appears at the bottom right of the image.

You can upload images to the 'Image bank', including digital photographs or images drawn and scanned into the computer. Click on 'Our images' and then 'Add' to navigate to where the image is stored. A thumbnail picture will be added to the gallery.

Writing your own story

Each CD-ROM contains a selection of blank writing templates. The fiction genre templates will be categorised under the button 'My story' and the non-fiction templates will be categorised under 'My recount' or 'My writing'. The writing templates encourage the children to produce an extended piece of genre writing. They can also add images, speech bubbles and use other tools to enhance their work.

The fiction titles also include a cover template for the children to use. They can customise their cover by adding their own title, blurb and images.

Section 1

Using good examples

Adventure story features

Plot
- Exciting and fast-moving, but with some varied pace.
- Includes problems and dilemmas.
- Often includes a surprise at the end.

Character
- A villain who is subtle, sneaky and mean.
- A hero we empathise with and want to succeed.

Setting
- Anywhere, at any time, but somewhere with the potential for danger or threat.

Language
- Combines action, dialogue and description.
- Uses powerful verbs to describe action, thoughts and feelings.
- Includes connectives to signal shifts of time or attention.
- Often includes similes.
- Uses well-chosen adverbs and adjectives.

What is an adventure story?

Adventure stories are written to entertain and enthral, allowing us to escape from reality. These are stories of heroes and villains, of dangerous quests, of strength and determination overcoming adversity. The most common structure is a chronological narrative, with excitement building as the hero faces danger. Much of the tension comes from the reader predicting what is likely to go wrong for the hero or heroine and how they will overcome challenges. Strong and interesting main characters, with whom we can identify, are placed in difficult or risky situations, facing physical or psychological challenges. Excitement and tension are built up through changes of pace, as main characters: are trapped but escape in the nick of time; chase and are chased; or confront their enemies. Often, just when we think all is well, another problem arises. Longer stories build tension in waves. One problem after another accelerates the adventure in several sections, with 'cliffhanger' endings sometimes used to build the tension along the way, making us want to read on.

Media adventure stories

Many children will have a rich experience of the adventure genre from the media and it is important to draw on this. Film and television narratives can be used to describe action, tension and excitement. You may find it useful to look at a short extract from a film to give more clues about the characteristics of adventure stories and to develop ideas for settings. Other key elements of the genre can be gathered from superhero comics and graphic novels. Children may also be familiar with ICT-based adventure games, where the structure often allows the user to select different routes through the order of events, involving them in deciding the fate of the protagonists.

Links to the Primary Framework

With the opportunity to create well-developed characters, exciting action and unexpected events, adventure stories also allow children to exercise their imagination. Adventure stories form the basis for the PNS Framework Unit 3 for Year 3 'Adventure and mystery' and could be incorporated into Unit 2 'Myths and legends' especially where quests are involved. In Year 4, adventure could be the basis for working on Unit 2, 'Stories set in imaginary worlds'.

Extract 1: The Catcher

What's on the CD-ROM

The Catcher
- Text extract to display and discuss.

Who was that?
- Drag and drop words under the correct headings.

This extract provides an example of a 'trigger event'. Polly is a lonely girl in a hidden/secret world and this describes her first sighting of the much-feared Catcher.

- Before reading, explain how Polly has been dancing ('twizzling') with an imaginary partner.

- Display the extract from the CD-ROM and highlight key features of the adventure genre. Point out the use of the senses in the first paragraph to create intrigue and suspense, the use of questions to help us to identify with Polly's feelings, how dialogue has been used to add interest and how the pace varies between fast and slow.

- Find examples of how language has been used, such as the powerful verbs, specific punctuation that helps us know how to read and interpret the text, and effective use of well-chosen adjectives, particularly those used to describe the Catcher.

- Open 'Who was that?' from the CD-ROM. Demonstrate how to drag and drop the words into the box to describe what Polly sees, hears or feels. The children can either complete this on screen or use photocopiable page 14. Let them finish by writing one or two suggestions for what might happen next in the story and discuss them later.

Extract 2: So Near...

What's on the CD-ROM

So Near...
- Text extract to display and discuss.

Time to decide
- A drag and drop activity to consider Salesse's decision.

In this extract, typical of a quest narrative, we see the confrontation, after a long and dangerous journey, between Salesse, the heroine, and Plotnik, the villain.

- Open the extract from the CD-ROM and highlight and discuss the techniques the writer uses, including dialogue, to convey the character of Plotnik. Encourage the children to read out Plotnik's words, putting expression and menace into his voice.

- Discuss how the pace of the action is sped up by the use of short sentences as the tiger arrives.

- Find examples of where the writer has used the senses, describing sounds, sights and physical feelings.

- Draw the children's attention to the unexpected appearance of the tiger, causing yet another problem for the heroine.

- Open 'Time to decide' from the CD-ROM and demonstrate how to drag and drop the statements linked to the decisions to stay or go.

- The children can complete this activity on screen or use photocopiable page 15.

- Choose a child to act as Salesse, to walk through 'conscience alley', while the other children line up on either side trying to persuade her to make either one decision or the other.

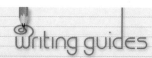

Extract 3: Joby and the Wasters

What's on the CD-ROM

Joby and the Wasters
- Text extract to display, discuss and edit.

This extract uses several typical adventure story features. There is the chase, when the hero, Joby, is pursued by the villains, the Wasters; tension when he seems to have found a way out, only to be thwarted; and a cliffhanger ending.

- Open the extract 'Joby and the Wasters' from the CD-ROM and discuss key features, such as the chase, the way the writer has built tension, the use of questions to engage the reader, the different sentence lengths and the cliffhanger ending.

- What do the children think of the newly introduced character – the old man? Whose side is he likely to be on?

- Demonstrate that the text can be edited: adding something before the start of the extract, incorporating adverbs, adjectives, dialogue or similes; change the font to add emphasis or create tension; or continue the story. Invite the children to work on the text themselves in the same way, on screen or by using photocopiable pages 12 and 13.

- As a further activity to support the children's understanding of key features, give them copies of the extract on photocopiable pages 12 and 13 and the activity 'Story detectives' on photocopiable page 16. Working in pairs they should find evidence in the text to complete each box.

Poster: Adventure soup

What's on the CD-ROM

Adventure soup
- Roll over the headings to reveal more information.

How does it feel?
- Drag and drop sentences to consider the effects of events on the reader.

The poster outlines some of the main features of adventure stories and is a guide that can be used throughout these activities.

- Open 'Adventure soup' from the CD-ROM. Roll over the text to reveal more information about each heading. Discuss each ingredient of an adventure story and the method for incorporating them, ready for when the children create a story of their own.

- Next, give pairs of children a copy of one of the three text extracts. Give the children access to the poster, either on screen or photocopiable page 18. Ask them to identify the ingredients from the poster on the text extract.

- Print and enlarge the poster for the children to use when planning, as a reminder of what has been learned, or to evaluate their own or each other's stories.

- To develop the children's understanding of how to engage the reader further in their adventure story, invite them to use the CD-ROM activity 'How does it feel?' to think about the effects of specific events on the reader. Encourage them to link this with the 'Trigger', 'Danger' and 'Suspense' ingredients on the poster.

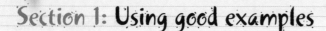
Extract 1: The Catcher

Breathless she came to a halt, and bowed to her invisible partner. Then, above the sound of her own breathing she heard a rustling and snapping of twigs, and looked into the copse beyond and saw a figure go striding by. It was there and gone in a trice, hidden by the trees, but Polly saw it for long enough to know that this was no ordinary visitor, come to feed the birds or walk the dog.

The man (for she saw that it was a man) went with long bounding strides – scissoring through the bracken – and yet there was a curious dreamlike slowness to his movements, as in a film show in slow motion. He might have been treading on air. And raised in his right arm was a long rod and a –

"Net?" Polly shook her head to settle it. Who would go striding through the woods at evening with a huge net, as if to catch some mysterious quarry?

"Not for butterflies," she thought, "nor even birds. Much too big."

Again she shook her head.

"Must've dreamed it," she thought. "All that twizzling."

From *The Secret World of Polly Flint* by Helen Cresswell

Extract 2: So Near...

'So, you have come for the secret formula,' smirked Plotnik. 'And what makes you think you will succeed where others have failed?' But even as he spoke he pressed a button on the desk in front of him, and a large panel in the wall on Salesse's right clicked and groaned open.

There was a bright piercing light, making Salesse catch her breath, when suddenly an enormous tiger sprang, snarling into the room. Its vicious teeth looked huge in its gaping mouth. Its roar was deafening. Its razor-sharp claws scratched marks on the tiled floor. Then slowly the tiger began to pad menacingly around the space between Salesse and Plotnik's desk. She could smell its foul breath and there were traces of its last meal still clinging to the fur around its mouth. On the desk the precious document that Salesse had searched for, against so many odds and for so long could be clearly seen. She felt her heart stop for a second, her mouth went dry and her palms became clammy with sweat. She knew that to save her friend's life, she must get that formula.

Plotnik beckoned with his leather-gloved finger, his green eyes narrowing in the smirk of a smile, urging Salesse forward.

'Come here then girl, it's yours for the taking. What are you waiting for?'

Illustration © 2010, Garry Davies.

Extract 3: Joby and the Wasters

Joby ran. Somewhere behind him, he heard a heavy door slam. He did not look back. He knew that longer legs than his were following, getting closer by the second, and he could not risk being caught; so he ran. His feet echoed on the stone floor, his breath came in sharp gasps, stabbing his insides. But still he ran, faster now. Would there be a way out? The question bounced off the inside of his skull and Joby answered it with his feet. He would find a way, he must find a way. So he ran with the rhythm, each foot thumping its beat on the floor. The corridor turned first left, then right until finally, at the end – there was a door! This must be it – his escape route!

Joby gasped little sighs of relief as he rushed towards the door. He reached out, grasped the handle and turned it, even in his haste imagining what might be on the other side. It seemed very stiff, as though it had been closed for a long time. Desperately he tried again, sucking in air, rattling the handle frantically. No good! In the short silences between his heartbeats he could hear heavy, running footsteps getting nearer in the corridor behind him. He turned around, but could see no one – yet. What could he do now? If he went back, he'd run straight into the hard grasping hands of the Wasters.

And then he heard a voice from the other side of the door.

 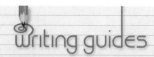

'Who dares to disturb me at this time of the night?' it demanded as a key turned in the lock. The door creaked open to reveal an old man, his shoulders hunched, his face half-hidden in the gloom. Watery grey eyes looked up towards Joby.

'You'd better come in, whoever you are,' he croaked.

Hesitantly, but with no other choice, Joby entered the room and the door was closed behind him.

Who was that?

● Polly Flint has just watched the mysterious Catcher passing by. How does Helen Cresswell describe this event?

What does Polly hear?

What does she see?

What might happen next?

How do you think Polly feels?

Illustration © 2002, Garry Davies.

Time to decide

● Salesse has to get past the tiger to get the secret formula or maybe she should just go back home. How would she feel if she turned back now? What will happen if she goes forward? Complete the speech bubbles.

If I turn back now...

If I go on now...

● Read the statements below. Write them under the correct headings.

If she goes on	If she turns back

She will live.

Her friend might die.

She will have failed.

She will feel disappointed.

She may succeed.

She might die.

She might have a plan.

She will feel proud.

Help may arrive.

Something might happen to the tiger.

She may outwit Plotnik.

She would be safe.

● What do you think Salesse will do, and what would happen next? Discuss with your partner.

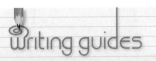

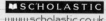
Story detectives

● How good a story detective are you? Use the extract about Joby and the Wasters to hunt for evidence of how the author has used some key features of an adventure story.

Questions to engage the reader	Short sentences to keep up the pace
Powerful verbs	A cliffhanger ending
An unexpected event	Use of dialogue

What might happen next to Joby, so that he isn't caught by the Wasters?

How does it feel?

● A good adventure story entertains the reader. Think of different ways of doing this to complete the strips on the right. The first two have been done for you. How do you want your reader to feel?

You introduce a mysterious character…	…the reader wants to know who it is.
The main character is in danger…	…the reader is worried.
The setting is dark and cold…	…the reader feels _____ _____
The journey is long and difficult…	…the reader _____ _____
Your main character is being chased…	…the reader _____ _____
Your main character returns home….	…the reader _____ _____

Illustrations © 2002, Garry Davies.

Adventure soup

serves many readers – ideal for entertaining

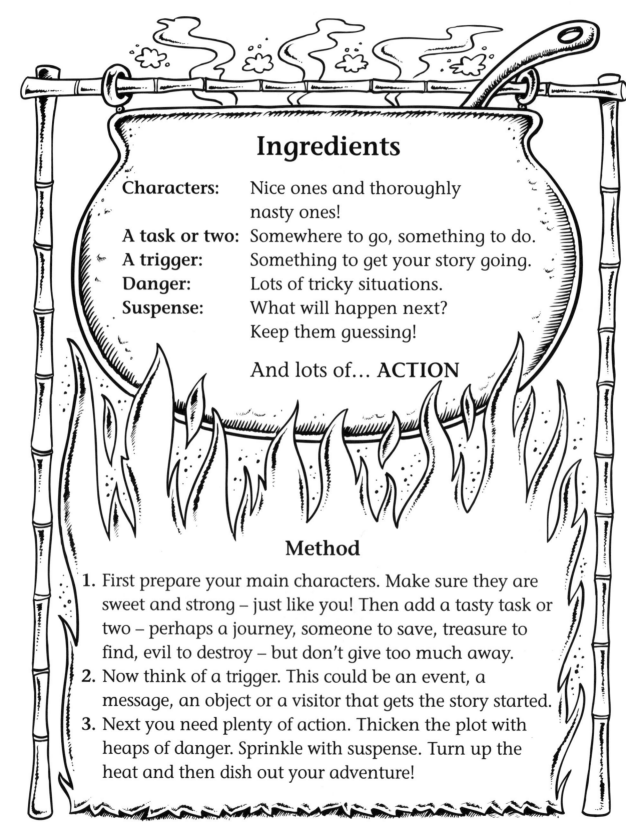

Ingredients

Characters: Nice ones and thoroughly nasty ones!

A task or two: Somewhere to go, something to do.

A trigger: Something to get your story going.

Danger: Lots of tricky situations.

Suspense: What will happen next? Keep them guessing!

And lots of... **ACTION**

Method

1. First prepare your main characters. Make sure they are sweet and strong – just like you! Then add a tasty task or two – perhaps a journey, someone to save, treasure to find, evil to destroy – but don't give too much away.
2. Now think of a trigger. This could be an event, a message, an object or a visitor that gets the story started.
3. Next you need plenty of action. Thicken the plot with heaps of danger. Sprinkle with suspense. Turn up the heat and then dish out your adventure!

Illustration © 2002, Garry Davies.

Section 2
Developing writing

This section will develop the children's awareness of how to work with the key features of adventure stories and guide them through the planning process, taking into account plot, character and setting. Note that while the 'hero' is often referred to, this could equally be a heroine.

Writer's knowledge

Whether working individually or with a writing partner, the children will be building up their own 'toolbox' of knowledge and skills about the genre, so that when they write they have the necessary ingredients to make their story successful. They will be developing their 'writer's knowledge', building on the activities from Section 1 where they were becoming familiar with the key features of the genre. Now they are ready to begin to develop and use what they have learned.

Thinking about writing

Before starting to write, it is important for the children to focus their thinking about key areas, such as plot, character and setting, and to practise specific techniques, without losing sight of the overall story. Do they know how their story will end, for instance? Shared writing, paired work, whole-class and group discussion are key in guiding this thinking process and the activities in this section are designed to support this.

Key features

Adventure stories need a good plot structure with scope for action and excitement. The children will also need to think about how their chosen setting links with their plot, bearing in mind things such as time of day and year or what the weather is like. They will need guidance in how to create opposing good and bad characters who grab the reader's attention so that we feel sympathy towards the hero – we really want them to succeed. Developing use of the senses will heighten the tension in an adventure story, as will the judicious use of questions – *What was that noise?* Knowing how to slow down the pace by using description or dialogue is another item for their writer's toolbox that works particularly well in adventure stories, where the action is usually fast-paced. Being armed with a bank of connectives could be useful – 'suddenly', 'meanwhile', 'at that very moment', 'later that night', 'without warning' and so on. Planning for a surprise at the end will keep the reader involved right to the finish – maybe a minor character turns out to save the day, for instance.

Activity breakdown

Planning
- Adventurous ideas (page 20)
- Adventure maps (page 20)
- Pull the trigger (page 21)
- Cliffhangers (page 21)

Plot
- An element of surprise (page 22)
- Meanwhile... (page 22)
- Should I stay or should I go? (page 23)
- Road rage (page 23)

Setting
- On location (page 24)

Character
- Seeing stars (page 24)

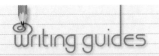

Activity 1: Adventurous ideas

Objective

To develop and refine ideas in writing using planning and problem-solving strategies. (Year 4 Strand 9)

What's on the CD-ROM

Media resources
- Sound effect to identify and discuss.

Adventure soup
- Roll over the headings to reveal more information.

What to do

This activity is designed to create a bridge between the familiarisation process from Section 1 and leading the children to think about and plan their own adventure story.

- Tell the children they will be building on what they learned from the activities in Section 1 to write some adventure stories.

- Play the sound effect from the CD-ROM. Ask the children to identify the sound (someone running) and suggest how it might relate to events in a quest, a chase or a fighting-evil adventure story. Gather as many possibilities as you can, developing the discussion to think about what might have led up to this part of the story and what might happen next.

- Using photocopiable page 25 'Adventurous ideas' ask pairs of children to decide on some scenarios of their own for each of these three types of adventure. (You may wish to enlarge this sheet to A3.) When they have completed the activity, they can select one of their ideas to write either an opening paragraph or a scene from the middle of the story.

- Afterwards, open the poster 'Adventure soup' from the CD-ROM (or photocopiable page 18) and ask the children to identify the elements of an adventure story that they have just worked on and what else would have to be planned.

Activity 2: Adventure maps

Objective

To develop and refine ideas in writing using planning and problem-solving strategies. (Year 4 Strand 9)

What's on the CD-ROM

Adventure maps
- Drag and drop features on to a map.

Media resources
- Discuss the image 'Hairpins'.

What to do

This activity will help the children to think about settings for their adventure story. It shows how several locations can be used, thus keeping up the pace and maintaining the reader's interest.

- Open the image 'Hairpins' from the CD-ROM and discuss how it might feature in an adventure story.

- Open 'Adventure maps' from the CD-ROM. Explain how maps, such as the endpapers from *The Hobbit* by JRR Tolkien, can be used to plan an adventure story, to choose settings or devise the plot.

- Show how the labelled features can be dragged and dropped onto the map outline. Talk about what might happen to characters in this landscape.

- Choose children to select and place features on the map and discuss how this environment could influence their stories. Use the final map to talk about how the story might travel from one location to another.

- Hand out photocopiable page 26 'Adventure maps' and ask the children to work in pairs. Together, the children should create their own adventure map. When they have completed this, they can make a note of some possible story events.

 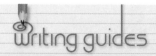

Activity 3: Pull the trigger

Objective

To identify features that writers use to provoke readers' reactions. (Year 3 Strand 8)

What's on the CD-ROM

Adventure soup
- Roll over the elements to display key features.

The Catcher
- Text extract to display and discuss.

What to do

This activity demonstrates how the story can be moved forward by using key 'trigger' events, which the hero or heroine must react to, thus changing the direction of the story.

- Open the poster 'Adventure soup' from the CD-ROM to remind the children about the characteristics of adventure stories, focussing on 'trigger' events. Explain that the trigger is the starting or turning point in the story, setting events in motion.

- Explain that you are going to collect examples of different types of triggers. Using the extract 'The Catcher' from the CD-ROM (or photocopiable page 10) identify the trigger, where Polly sees the figure of a man with a net, and explain that this is an event that changes what she was originally doing.

- Talk about messages that act as triggers, such as phone calls, text or emails. In pairs, ask the children to jot down ideas for a trigger message on photocopiable page 27 'Pull the trigger'. Discuss some of their ideas, then repeat the exercise for 'Object' (such as a parcel, scroll or map) and 'Visitor' (such as an old friend or a strange tall man with a bad cough).

- Invite pairs of children to improvise some of the trigger events as a drama activity.

Activity 4: Cliffhangers

Objective

To identify features that writers use to provoke readers' reactions. (Year 3 Strand 8)

What's on the CD-ROM

Joby and the Wasters
- Text extract for display and discussion.

Cliffhangers
- Choose a scenario and type the solution.

What to do

This activity introduces the device of using a cliffhanger ending to retain reader interest and provide tension points in the story.

- Open 'Joby and the Wasters' from the CD-ROM and show how the writer uses a cliffhanger ending, leaving the hero in a tricky situation, encouraging the reader to predict what might happen. Emphasise that the writer knows how things will work out, but the reader doesn't!

- Explain how writers use cliffhangers to increase excitement and drama. Ask the children for examples from familiar TV programmes.

- Open 'Cliffhangers' from the CD-ROM and explain that it contains a series of cliffhangers for the children to resolve. Complete one as an example before the children do the activity, on screen or using photocopiable page 28.

- Afterwards, choose an example of a couple of short paragraphs for shared writing. Demonstrate how to use language and sentence construction to build up tension and to make the writing flow.

- Ask the children to select a different scenario, either one of their own or one from the previously completed activity, to write as a fully developed cliffhanger ending.

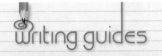

Activity 5: An element of surprise

Objective

To show imagination through the language used to create atmosphere or suspense.
(Year 4 Strand 9)

What to do

Working well as a guided writing activity, this will help children to think about specific events in their adventure stories that, by involving changes of mood and pace, surprise and grip the reader.

● Ask the children to talk about occasions when they have been surprised or frightened, thinking about how they felt before and after the incident. Use an example of your own to start the discussion.

● On an enlarged version of photocopiable page 29 'An element of surprise', use one of the suggestions from the discussion as the surprise to demonstrate how to complete the sheet.

● Ask the children to put this idea into an adventure story context, encouraging them to think about giving a false sense of security – how an adventure hero may be resting, sleeping or walking without a care when suddenly something happens to change the mood.

● Talk about the atmosphere before and after (what the hero can hear, see and feel).

● Ask the children to jot their ideas on the photocopiable sheet, then discuss these, talking about ways of increasing the element of surprise. Invite the children to write their own surprise scene in continuous prose.

Activity 6: Meanwhile...

Objective

To use settings and characterisation to engage readers' interest.
(Year 4 Strand 9)

What's on the CD-ROM

Media resources
● Use the 'Polar explorers' image as a discussion and drama stimulus.

What to do

This activity helps children to develop tension in their adventure stories by recounting events that are happening at the same time.

● Open the image 'Polar explorers' from the CD-ROM and discuss the fact that both events are happening at the same time.

● Ask pairs of children to freeze-frame the scenes and talk about their contrasting thoughts. Concentrate on the characters' feelings – what are they thinking and hoping at this moment? Could anything happen to change the seemingly inevitable course of events?

● Can the children think of any other examples from stories, TV or film, where two things are happening at the same time? For example, the hero could be imprisoned, trapped or tied up while the enemy is near to completing the quest or finding the treasure.

● Make a list on the board of a few of the children's ideas, so they can refer to this if necessary during the next part of the activity.

● Ask the children to complete photocopiable page 30 'Meanwhile...', sketching scenes on the left and making notes on the right. Draw their attention to the connecting words and phrases that emphasise two events occurring simultaneously.

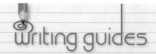

Activity 7: Should I stay or should I go?

Objective

To write narratives in which events are sequenced logically and conflicts resolved.
(Year 3 Strand 9)

What's on the CD-ROM

Should I stay or should I go?
- Roll over the 'Yes' and 'No' to reveal possible outcomes.

What to do

This activity will encourage the children to consider more than one possible outcome for events in their adventure stories.

- Explain how characters in an adventure story are often faced with a dilemma or difficult choice and that what they decide affects how the story continues. Ask for examples from stories, TV programmes or films that the children know.

- Open 'Should I stay or should I go?' from the CD-ROM. Discuss the first scenario, eliciting possible outcomes, before rolling over 'Yes' and 'No' to reveal two suggestions, both of which would fit logically in the context of an adventure story and would carry the story on to the next event. The four other scenarios work in the same way and can be used either for whole-class or paired and individual use.

- Alternatively, let the children use photocopiable page 31 'Should I stay or should I go?' to work independently, cutting and pasting each of the scenarios and writing their own yes/no options.

- As an extension activity, encourage the children to write a short excerpt based on one of the dilemmas, or rehearse and perform a chosen scenario, with both outcomes, to the class.

Activity 8: Road rage

Objective

To develop and refine ideas in writing using planning and problem-solving strategies.
(Year 4 Strand 9)

What's on the CD-ROM

Road rage
- A roll-over activity to prompt solutions to problems.

What to do

This activity shows the children how using a chase scene in their adventure can vary pace and introduce excitement.

- Talk about chase scenes in films the children have seen. Watch a video extract in preparation, if possible.

- Explain how chase scenes vary pace and introduce excitement through fast action and changing fortunes.

- Open 'Road rage' from the CD-ROM and demonstrate how to roll over the coloured sections of road to reveal dilemmas. Invite solutions to the various setbacks that occur, stressing that there could be several possibilities. Invite pairs of children to work at the computer, discussing and jotting down their solutions to the problems encountered.

- Alternatively, let pairs of children use photocopiable page 32, with dice and counters, to play the game. Explain that if players hit a shaded area, they must throw the dice again to identify a 'setback' to face. As they wait their next turn, they must note down a solution that they read out before their next turn in order to rejoin the game.

- The written solutions can be used in shared writing to compose a chase extract from an adventure story, using powerful verbs and exciting vocabulary.

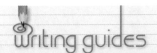

Activity 9: On location

Objective

To use settings to engage readers' interest.
(Year 4 Strand 9)

What's on the CD-ROM

Media resources
- Use image 'Ruined building' to stimulate ideas for descriptive vocabulary.

What to do

This activity helps children to think about the settings they can use in adventure story writing and how describing these settings well can add to the atmosphere of the story.

- Open the image 'Ruined building' from the CD-ROM. Ask for suggestions about what this building might have been and what might still be inside it. List words and phrases from the children to describe what they see and what they can imagine. Include the building, the landscape and the atmosphere suggested by the weather.

- Discuss how this setting might be used as a location in an adventure story – what dangers could be lurking for the hero or heroine?

- Hand out photocopiable page 33 'On location' and ask pairs of children to write descriptive words and phrases for the locations listed. For example, for 'volcano' they may write 'belching fire and smoke', or for 'avalanche' it could be 'enormous boulders tumbling down'. Against 'secret doorway', they might write 'creaking rusty hinges' or 'heavy and stiff'. Choose some children to read their descriptions for others to guess the location being described.

- Working individually, ask the children to choose one of the locations as the basis for writing a descriptive paragraph. Encourage them to add other details, such as the weather or time of day.

Activity 10: Seeing stars

Objective

To use characterisation to engage readers' interest.
(Year 4 Strand 9)

What's on the CD-ROM

Media resources
- Image 'Dr Jekyll and Mr Hyde' for display and discussion.

Seeing stars
- Choose characters from 'These images'.
- Type descriptions of the characters.

What to do

This activity helps children to develop some adventure characters, to think of their attributes and the particular quest they are on.

- Open the image 'Dr Jekyll and Mr Hyde' from the CD-ROM. Explain how drinking a secret potion changed the character of Dr Jekyll into the villainous Mr Hyde and discuss character types.

- Open 'Seeing stars' from the CD-ROM and use it to model a character plan. For each hero and villain, complete the profiles with the children's help. Choose a hero and a villain from 'These images' in the 'Image bank' and then type aspects about the characters in the boxes.

- Give each child a copy of photocopiable page 34 'Seeing stars' to create their own hero or heroine and villain. The heroine, for example, could be on a quest to find Egyptian treasures. She could be an expert in desert survival and reading hieroglyphs, but her weakness might be a fear of heights. Talk about how her strengths could feature in an adventure story, and how any flaws she has could be used to add interest and tension and help the reader identify with her as a real person. Follow the same type of process for the villain.

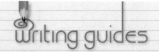

Adventurous ideas

● Gather some ideas for adventure stories. What type of adventure might you have and what might happen to your hero or heroine?

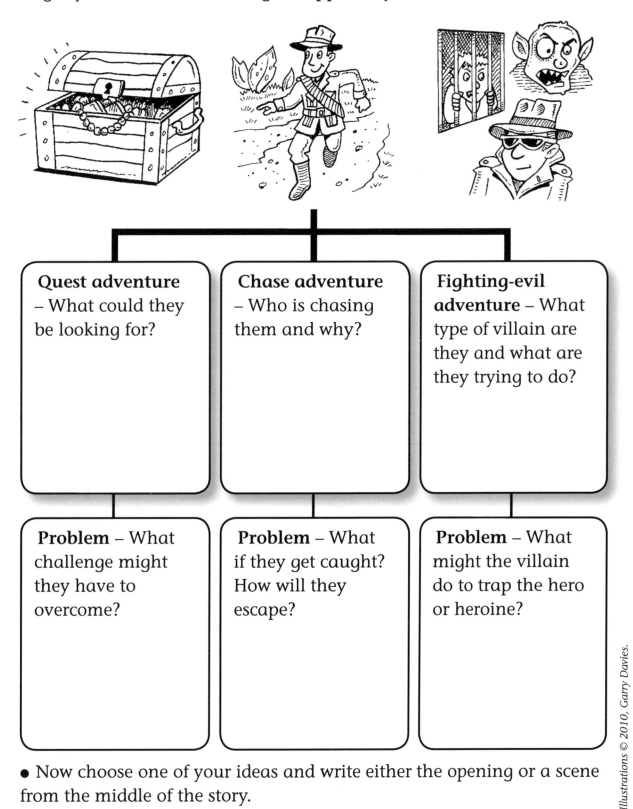

Quest adventure – What could they be looking for?

Chase adventure – Who is chasing them and why?

Fighting-evil adventure – What type of villain are they and what are they trying to do?

Problem – What challenge might they have to overcome?

Problem – What if they get caught? How will they escape?

Problem – What might the villain do to trap the hero or heroine?

● Now choose one of your ideas and write either the opening or a scene from the middle of the story.

Illustrations © 2010, Garry Davies.

Adventure maps

● Create your own adventure map! Use some of the features below and draw them on to your map. Label them with names of your own. You can use your map to work out some of the events in your adventure story.

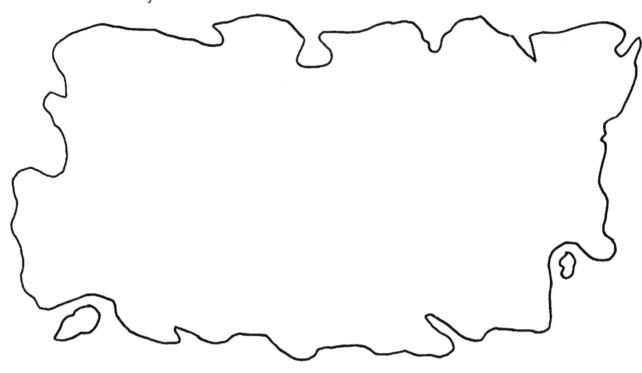

Fast-flowing river	Ruined temple	Sea cliffs	Cave	A forest
A mountain range	A deserted village	A wrecked ship	An airstrip	Quicksand

Illustrations © 2010, Garry Davies.

Pull the trigger

● What events can you list that would trigger a change in an adventure story? Some examples have been given to help you.

Event

The hero's car breaks down.

Message

The heroine receives an invitation to a party.

Object

The hero finds an old map in a rusty box in the garden shed.

Visitor

A mysterious old lady buys a house in the village.

Photocopiable **SCHOLASTIC** www.scholastic.co.uk

Cliffhangers

● Place your hero or heroine in a tricky situation. How much you tell the reader about the situation and how much you don't will help to make your adventure story exciting. Read this example, then think of some tricky situations of your own.

● Choose one of them to write as a passage.

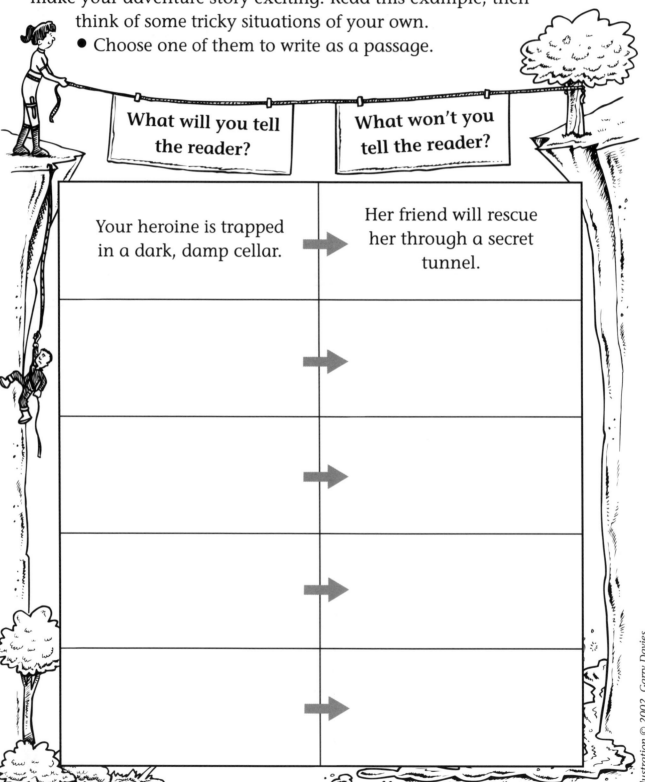

What will you tell the reader?	What won't you tell the reader?
Your heroine is trapped in a dark, damp cellar.	Her friend will rescue her through a secret tunnel.

Illustration © 2002, Garry Davies.

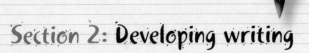
An element of surprise

● Think about how you will surprise your reader, for example, a door bursts open, your hero falls through a trapdoor, or the villain attacks. What happens before and after the surprise event?

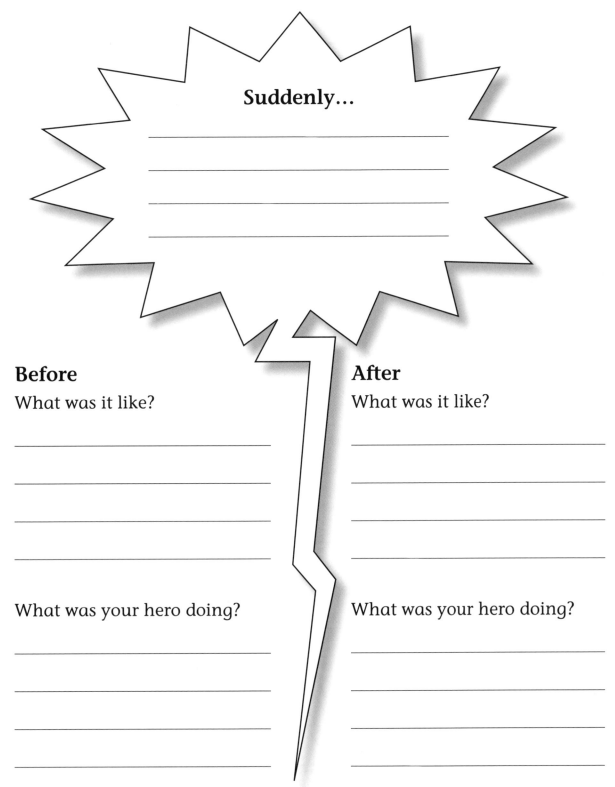

Suddenly...

_____

_____

_____

_____

Before

What was it like?

_____

_____

_____

What was your hero doing?

_____

_____

_____

After

What was it like?

_____

_____

_____

What was your hero doing?

_____

_____

_____

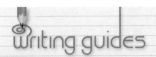

Meanwhile...

● Sometimes two things will be happening at the same time in your adventure story. Perhaps your heroine is trapped just as the villain is about to find the treasure. Sketch two events in the boxes and describe what is going on. Join the two events with words like:

| at the same time | meanwhile | while this was going on |

Event 1

Writer's notebook

Event 2

Illustration © 2002, Garry Davies.

Should I stay or should I go?

● Sometimes your hero or heroine will be faced with a difficult choice – a choice where there is possible DANGER! Cut out the four pictures below and think of good and bad consequences, like those in the example.

Road rage

● Imagine you are a character in an adventure story and you are being chased. Choose your vehicle! Throw the dice. If you land on a shaded square, throw the dice again to select the setback. Miss a turn while you jot down a solution to the problem. Read out your solution to get back on the road when it's your turn again.

Finish

1 Flat tyre. You skid off the road!

2 Rock fall. Your vehicle crashes!

3 Fireball. You brake suddenly!

4 Ice on the road. You hit a tree!

5 Wounded in the arm. You lose control!

Start

6 Out of fuel. You grind to a halt!

Illustration © 2002, Garry Davies.

On location

● Setting is important for an adventure story. You will need a dramatic landscape with lots of natural dangers and buildings that are full of surprises, secrets and mysteries. Underline two or three features from each list and make notes on how you could use them in your story.

tropical rainforest

sandy desert

deep ravine

volcano

cliff face

fast-flowing river

quicksand

winding road

avalanche

secret doorway

underground passage

trapdoor

wall paintings

remote castle

crumbling pillars

abandoned temple

ancient tomb

Seeing stars

● Adventure stories need star characters. They need good characters (heroes and heroines) and bad characters (villains). Heroes have a task to achieve – villains get in the way!

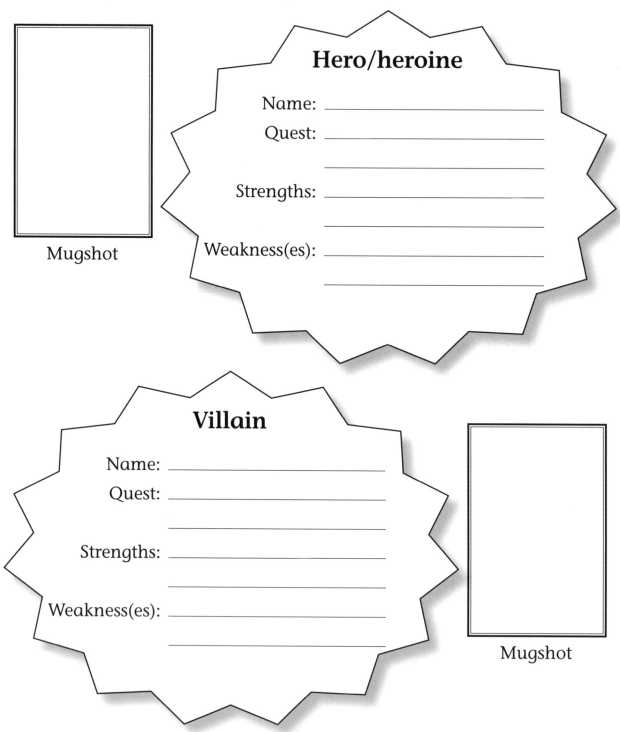

Mugshot

Hero/heroine

Name: _____

Quest: _____

_____

Strengths: _____

_____

Weakness(es): _____

_____

Villain

Name: _____

Quest: _____

_____

Strengths: _____

_____

Weakness(es): _____

_____

Mugshot

● Now give a short history of both these characters.

Section 3

Writing

The three extended writing projects in this section provide opportunities for the children to put everything they have learned about writing adventure stories into practice.

Each of the projects requires the children to plan and write a complete adventure story using narrative structures characteristic of the genre.

- Project 1, 'Dangerous quest' – the children plan and write a typical quest story.

- Project 2, 'Heroes and villains' – the children plan and write an adventure where a hero is pitted against a villain and is ultimately victorious.

- Project 3, 'Race to the finish' – the children will plan and write an adventure where the hero has to battle against natural hazards as well as a sneaky villain in order to complete a challenge.

Creating the stories

Each project includes specific guidance to lead the children towards completing a story, while letting them make their own choices. You need to allow several sessions to take the children through the planning, drafting, writing, editing and publishing process.

There will be activities from the previous sections that the children will find useful, so having access to their earlier work is recommended. Using these in conjunction with ideas from the CD-ROM, the children will be guided to devise plots, develop characters and organise their story. It would also be useful for each child to have a copy of the poster 'Adventure soup' (page 18) to remind them of key elements of the genre. Targeted support will be necessary for individuals as they write independently. All children should be encouraged to share their work with a writing partner, each saying what they like about their partner's work and offering any suggestions for how it might be improved.

When writing these stories, the children will be guided to consider how to present contrasting characters, how to use settings appropriate to the plot, and how to sequence their stories logically, varying pace and adding excitement as they go.

Using the writing templates

The writing templates provided on the CD-ROM allow the children to produce their own adventure stories using images and text. As well as composing the narrative for their story, the children can insert speech and thought bubbles, load their own images and design a cover for their finished story, which they can print out. Alternatively, you could print the blank layouts for the children to write on directly.

Writing tips

- Remember the stories should entertain – keep your reader in mind.
- Use powerful verbs to describe actions, thoughts and feelings.
- Use dialogue to bring the story to life and keep up the pace.
- Choose good adverbs and adjectives to write vivid descriptions.
- Include elements of surprise, exciting action and unexpected events.
- Create contrasting characters.

Project 1: Dangerous quest

Objective

To use beginning, middle and end to write narratives in which events are sequenced logically and conflicts resolved.
(Year 3 Strand 9)

What's on the CD-ROM

My adventure story
- Compose a quest story using the writing templates.

What to do

This project guides the children to plan and write a simple narrative based on the classic 'quest' theme and would fit in with work on Greek myths, for instance.

- Using photocopiable page 40 'Dangerous quest' guide the children through how to complete this outline, which helps them plan what their story is about, who the key characters are and what actually happens.

- Discuss possible objects for the quest, using familiar texts such as *Lord of the Rings* or *Jason and the Argonauts*.

- Discuss a background for the quest – which character in the story decided on it (perhaps the King, an anxious parent, a wizard or a worried village elder) and why the hero or heroine was selected (perhaps they were particularly strong and brave, had special powers, or had performed great feats before).

- Encourage them to think about time as well as place for the setting, for example, ancient Greece, a time in the future or any period in history that you are currently working on.

- The children may wish to use the hero they created for the 'Seeing stars' activity earlier (see page 24). Alternatively, they could use the same process to develop new characters, linked to the particular focus of this story.

- It may help if pairs of children work together when completing their individual plans. They should start by deciding on the object of the quest then complete the two linked boxes before thinking about the particular setting and the dangers and challenges of the quest narrative. They may wish to make a rough draft to talk over with a partner before completing a revised, more detailed plan, ready for when they begin writing.

- Once the plans are complete, the children are ready to use the 'My adventure story' writing frames on the CD-ROM to create their quest stories on screen.

- Demonstrate how to select the writing frame, add text and insert and resize images from the 'Image bank' then save and retrieve their work.

- Finished stories should be shared with a target audience, either as on-screen texts or in printed form (or both).

 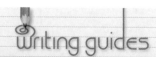

Project 2: Heroes and villains

Objective

To use beginning, middle and end to write narratives in which events are sequenced logically and conflicts resolved.
(Year 3 Strand 9)

What's on the CD-ROM

The confrontation
- A text-entry activity to plan dialogue.

Story planner
- Plan your story.

My adventure story
- Compose a story using the writing templates.

What to do
In this project, the hero encounters a villain in the course of the adventure, who is overcome so that the hero is victorious.

- Explain that in this adventure the hero has a villain to contend with. Open 'The confrontation' from the CD-ROM and discuss how dialogue can tell us more about the characters as well as keeping up the pace of the adventure. Type suggestions from the children in the boxes on screen. Give them a copy of photocopiable page 41, or let them work on screen, to write their own ideas.

- Next, open 'Story planner' from the CD-ROM and, using suggestions from the children, model how to complete it, reminding them of earlier activities to help them.

- Hand out photocopiable pages 38 and 39 'Story planner' for the children to plan their own story. They could use the 'Adventure maps' activity from Section 2 (page 20) to help create settings.

- When the story plans are completed, the children should talk through their story to a partner before beginning to write, and make any changes they think might be needed.

- The children are now ready to create their stories using the 'My adventure story' writing frames on the CD-ROM.

Project 3: Race to the finish

Objective

To use settings and characterisation to engage readers' interest.
(Year 4 Strand 9)

What's on the CD-ROM

Race to the finish
- Roll over the challenges to reveal hazards.

Story planner
- Plan your story.

My adventure story
- Compose a story using the writing templates.

What to do
For this project the children choose a race or action-adventure challenge, with the villain doing all they can to prevent the hero from winning.

- Open 'Race to the finish' from the CD-ROM. Discuss the possible races or action challenges that might happen in each of the settings. Next, roll over each setting to reveal a possible object that the villain might sabotage to hinder the hero's way. Talk about what the villain might do to the objects, and discuss how the hero might overcome them.

- Hand out photocopiable page 42 for the children to form their own ideas. When they have decided on the challenge for their adventure story, give each child a copy of photocopiable page 43 'Vital equipment' for them to consider what their hero would need to take on their adventure. Anticipating potential difficulties should anything go wrong with this vital equipment can then form part of their story.

- To help plan their story, provide the children with photocopiable pages 38 and 39 'Story planner', which you can model using the CD-ROM.

- With the planning complete, the children can create their stories using the 'My adventure story' writing frames and images on the CD-ROM.

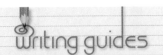

Story planner

● Use what you already know about adventure stories to think about and plan your own story, using this framework.

The hero
How will you make us like your hero or heroine?

The villain
Make us want the villain to lose!

The setting
List important and interesting things.

The trigger
What is the hero doing when the trigger occurs?

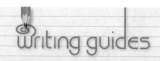

The hero solves a problem

What challenge, threat or obstacle is overcome, and how?

The hero and villain meet

Where and how do they meet? What happens?

The hero is victorious

How does the hero overcome the villain?

The final outcome

What happens in the end? What becomes of the villain?

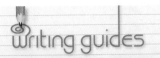

Dangerous quest

● Use this plan to capture your ideas before you start to write. Begin by deciding on the object of the quest. You could talk it over with a partner first.

What is the object of the quest, and what is special about it?

Why has the hero been chosen?

Why is the quest important, and to whom?

What is the setting for the story?

What dangers will the hero face on the quest?

How will the hero deal with the dangers?

The confrontation

● Using dialogue that fits your characters is a good way to bring your story to life and keep up the pace. Imagine your hero and villain meeting in your story. What might each of them say? There are a couple of ideas to help you get started. Jot down your own pieces of dialogue here for use later in the story.

The hero might say...

So! We meet at last!

The villain might say...

You will never get the better of me!

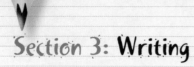
Race to the finish

● What adventurous race or competition will your hero take part in? What sneaky wiles will the villain come up with to stop your hero winning? You have been given a couple of ideas to start you off. Write your own ideas in the spaces below.

Adventure challenge	Possible hazard
A race through the jungle.	The villain cuts down trees to block the path through the jungle.
A car rally across the desert.	The villain sneaks into the hero's camp at night and steals the water supply.

● Now choose the one to use in your own story.

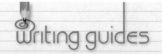

Vital equipment

● What will your hero need to pack for the adventure? The pictures will give you some ideas, but you may think of your own. Why will the equipment be needed and what could go wrong with it?

Equipment	Why it's needed	What could go wrong with it?

Illustration © 2010, Garry Davies.

Review

This section offers the opportunity to evaluate how well the children have incorporated their prior learning into their writing. It is important for the children as well as the teacher to engage in this reflective process, which should be guided by success criteria linked to the specific learning objectives listed.

Self review

Photocopiable page 45 can act as a set of success criteria to guide the children while they work on their stories. When the stories are finished, the completed grid should record how well the children think they have covered the listed features. Discussion while they are completing the grid could include questions to guide reflection, such as 'Tell me some of the ways you made your hero and villain different' or 'Show me where you have used the senses in a description'.

Peer review

Peer review forms part of the process of a collaborative approach to writing. Photocopiable page 46 will guide the children to provide a positive response to others' work and can be the basis for paired discussion.

Teacher review

When assessing the children's writing, look for evidence to show that they have made specific word choices designed to show the difference between their key characters. Have they included dialogue that fits each character? Does the setting match the adventure? Have they used adjectives judiciously and are they balanced by the use of powerful verbs and well-chosen adverbs? Have they used the idea of a trigger event and does it have a direct effect on the plot? Is there a cliffhanger in the story and does it get resolved? Overall, does the story entertain and enthral? On the technical side, look out for correct punctuation, including the use of speech marks, question marks and exclamation marks.

The teacher review sheet on photocopiable page 47 covers the Assessment Focuses for writing that link to this writing guide. It can be used both formatively and summatively, with evidence being taken from any of the activities. You can compare your assessment with the child's own perceptions, noting any differences and using this to inform discussions with them.

Used as a tool for ongoing assessment, this grid can both highlight gaps and identify good progress, so informing the next steps for learning. You may wish to revisit some of the activities in Section 2 for some children, perhaps in guided writing group sessions, where closer attention can be given to individual needs.

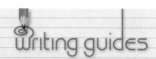

Self review

- Tick one of the boxes for each statement listed below.

		Not at all 😦	A little 😐	Quite well 🙂	Very well 😊
Characters	A reader can tell the difference between my hero and villain because of how I describe them and what they do.				
	The dialogue I have written for each of my characters helps a reader to know what they are like.				
Settings	The setting I have chosen fits the adventure well.				
	I have used my senses to describe the setting and included details about the time and the weather.				
Plot	My story gives a reason for the adventure and includes a challenge for the hero.				
	I have included a trigger event that has an effect on what the hero does and a cliffhanger.				
Language	I have used adjectives, powerful verbs and adverbs to describe people, places and events.				
	I have used connectives to signal changes of time or characters' attention.				

The best thing about my story was:

_____

I could make my story even better by:

_____

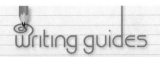
Writing guides

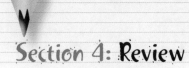

Peer review

● Help your partner to evaluate their adventure story by answering these questions.

What did you enjoy most about the story?

_____

_____

_____

Who was your favourite character and why?

_____

_____

_____

Which was the most exciting part?

_____

_____

_____

Write down any words, phrases or sentences that you thought worked really well.

_____

_____

_____

How could the story be made even better?

_____

_____

_____

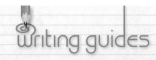

Writing guides

Teacher review

	AF5 Vary sentences for clarity, purpose and effect.	AF6 Write with technical accuracy of syntax and punctuation in phrases, clauses and sentences.	AF3 Organise and present whole texts effectively, sequencing and structuring information, ideas and events.	AF4 Construct paragraphs and use cohesion within and between paragraphs.	AF1 Write imaginative, interesting and thoughtful texts.	AF2 Produce texts which are appropriate to task, reader and purpose.	AF7 Select appropriate and effective vocabulary.
LEVEL 2	Past and present tense generally consistent. *Use interesting vocabulary varying the use of verbs for effect, keeping the tense consistent.* (Pupil Writing Target, level 2a)	Sentence demarcation with capital letters and full stops usually accurate. Some accurate use of question and exclamation marks.	Some basic sequencing of ideas or material, *for example, time-related words or phrases, line breaks, headings, numbers. Writing shows characteristics of chosen form based on structure of known texts.* (Pupil Writing Target, level 2c)	Ideas in sections grouped by content, some linking by simple pronouns.	Some apt word choices create interest. Brief comments, questions about events or actions suggest viewpoint.	Some appropriate features of the given form used. *Select and use vocabulary appropriate to different text types.* (Pupil Writing Target, level 2a)	Simple, often speech-like vocabulary conveys relevant meanings. Some adventurous word choices, *for example, opportune use of new vocabulary.*
LEVEL 3	*And, but, so are the most common connectives.*	Straightforward sentences usually demarcated accurately with full stops, capital letters, question and exclamation marks. Some, limited, use of speech punctuation.	Some attempt to organise ideas with related points placed next to each other. Some attempt to sequence ideas logically.	Within paragraphs/ sections, some links between sentences, *for example, use of pronouns or of adverbials.*	Some appropriate ideas and content included. Some attempt to elaborate on basic information or events, for example, nouns expanded by simple adjectives.	Some attempts at appropriate style, with attention to reader. *Use descriptive language to establish a specific setting in writing.* (Pupil Writing Target, level 3b) *Develop character in more detail in narrative writing.* (Pupil Writing Target, level 3a)	Some words selected for effect or occasion. *Use adjectives and adverbs to create variety and add interest for the reader.* (Pupil Writing Target, level 3b)

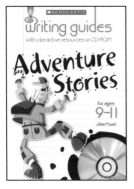